Music Theory Practice Paper 2021 Grade 1 A
Model Answers

1 Rhythm   /15

1.1 (a) $\frac{3}{4}$ (3)

(b) 𝄴

(c) $\frac{2}{4}$

1.2   (5)

(a)

(b)

(c)

(d)

(e)

1.3 (a) 3   (2)

(b) 16

1.4   (1)

1.5 (3)

1.6 (1)

2 Pitch   /15

2.1 (a) A   (b) F♯   (c) B♭   (7)

(d) E   (e) C♯   (f) G

(g) D

2.2 (4)

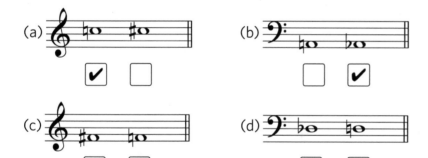

2.3 (a) 𝄢   (b) 𝄞   (c) 𝄞   (d) 𝄞   (4)

3 Keys and Scales   /15

3.1 (1)

3.2 (1)

3.3 (3)

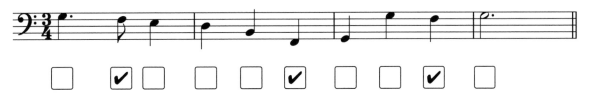

3.4 (2)

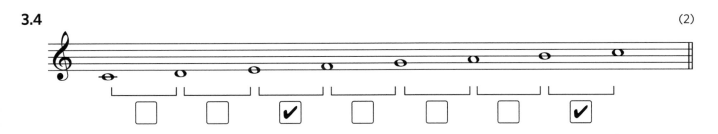

3.5 (a) **TRUE** (4)

(b) **FALSE**

(c) **FALSE**

(d) **TRUE**

3.6 (1)

3.7 TRUE (1)

3.8 (2)

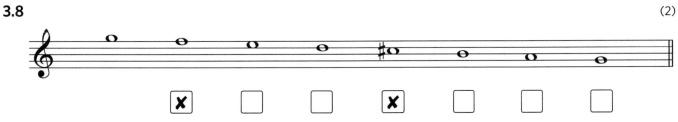

4 Intervals

4.1 (5)

4.2 (a) 4th   (b) 2nd   (c) 5th   (5)

(d) 3rd   (e) 7th

5 Tonic Triads

5.1 (a) **FALSE** (3)

(b) **FALSE**

(c) **TRUE**

5.2 (3)

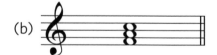

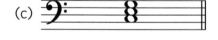

5.3 (a) C major (4)

(b) G major

(c) D major

(d) F major

6 Terms and Signs   /5

Allegro means:

quick

da capo means:

repeat from the beginning

mf means:

moderately loud

(5)

⌢ means:

pause on the note or rest

accelerando means:

gradually getting quicker

7 Music in Context   /5

7.1 FALSE   (1)

7.2 bar 5   (1)

7.3 (a) semibreve   (3)

 (b) bar 3

 (c) bar 7

Music Theory Practice Paper 2021 Grade 1 B
Model Answers

1 Rhythm

1.1 (a) $\frac{4}{4}$ (3)

    (b) $\frac{2}{4}$

    (c) $\frac{3}{4}$

1.2 (5)

(a)

(b)

(c)

(d)

(e)

1.3 (a) 3 (2)

    (b) 4

1.4 (1)

☐　　　　　　☐　　　　　　☑

8

1.5 (3)

1.6 (1)

2 Pitch /15

2.1 (a) G (b) F♯ (c) D (7)

(d) C♯ (e) E (f) F

(g) B♭

2.2 (4)

2.3 (a) (b) (c) (d) (4)

3 Keys and Scales /15

3.1 (1)

3.2 (1)

3.3 (3)

3.4 (2)

3.5 (a) **TRUE** (4)

(b) **FALSE**

(c) **TRUE**

(d) **FALSE**

3.6 (1)

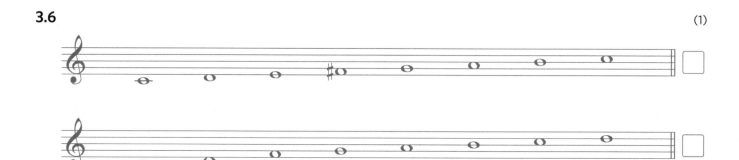

3.7 FALSE (1)

3.8 (2)

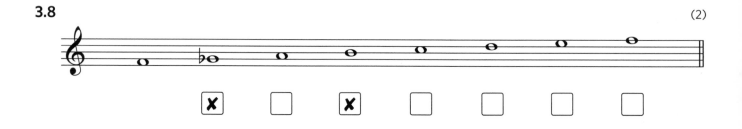

4 Intervals

4.1 (5)

4.2 (a) 3rd   (b) 4th   (c) 7th   (5)

(d) 2nd   (e) 6th

5 Tonic Triads

5.1 (a) **TRUE** (3)

(b) **FALSE**

(c) **TRUE**

5.2 (3)

(a) 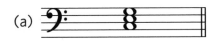   (b)    (c)

5.3 (a) F major (4)

(b) D major

(c) C major

(d) G major

6 Terms and Signs /5

Moderato means:

at a moderate pace

a tempo means:

in time

pp means:

very quiet

(5)

♩ = 60 means:

60 crotchet beats in a minute

means:

slur: perform smoothly

7 Music in Context /5

7.1 TRUE (1)

7.2 3 (1)

7.3 (a) dotted minim (3)

   (b) A

   (c) bar 3

Music Theory Practice Paper 2021 Grade 1 C
Model Answers

1 Rhythm

1.1 (a) $\frac{2}{4}$ (3)

(b) $\frac{4}{4}$

(c) $\frac{3}{4}$

1.2 (5)

1.3 (a) 6 (2)

(b) 4

1.4 (1)

1.5 (3)

1.6 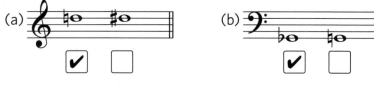 (1)

2 Pitch   /15

2.1 (a) B   (b) F♯   (c) C♯   (7)

(d) B♭   (e) E   (f) C

(g) C

2.2   (4)

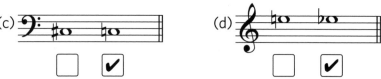

2.3 (a)   (b)   (c)   (d)   (4)

3 Keys and Scales   /15

3.1   (1)

3.2   (1)

3.3 (3)

☐   ✔   ☐   ☐   ☐   ✔   ☐   ☐   ✔   ☐

3.4 (2)

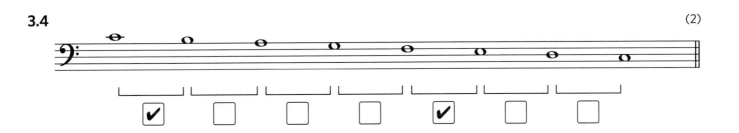

✔   ☐   ☐   ☐   ✔   ☐   ☐

3.5 (a) **FALSE** (4)

   (b) **TRUE**

   (c) **FALSE**

   (d) **TRUE**

3.6 (1)

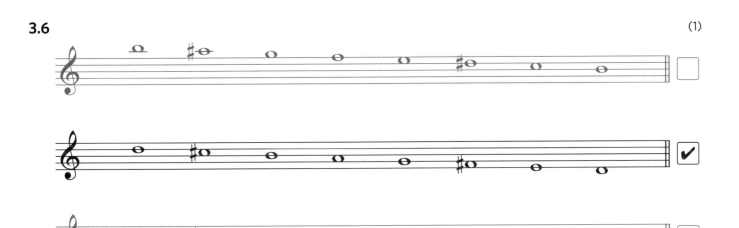

☐

✔

☐

3.7 TRUE (1)

3.8 (2)

☐   ☐   ✘   ☐   ☐   ✘   ☐

4 Intervals

/10

4.1

(5)

4.2 (a) 7th   (b) 3rd   (c) 4th   (5)

    (d) 6th   (e) 5th

5 Tonic Triads

/10

5.1 (a) **FALSE**   (3)

    (b) **TRUE**

    (c) **FALSE**

5.2 (3)

 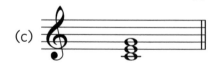

5.3 (a) D major   (4)

    (b) C major

    (c) F major

    (d) G major

6 Terms and Signs /5

Andante means:

at a medium speed

mf means:

moderately loud

legato means:

smoothly

(5)

⎯⎯⎯⎯⎯ means:

gradually getting quieter

⌢ means:

pause on the note or rest

7 Music in Context /5

7.1 FALSE (1)

7.2 4 (1)

7.3 (a) minim rest (3)

(b) G

(c) bar 7

Music Theory Practice Paper 2021 Grade 1 D
Model Answers

1 Rhythm   /15

1.1 (a) $\frac{3}{4}$ (3)

(b) $\frac{4}{4}$

(c) $\frac{2}{4}$

1.2   (5)

(a)

(b)

(c)

(d)

(e)

1.3 (a) 8   (2)

(b) 3

1.4   (1)

1.5 (3)

1.6 𝅝 𝅗𝅥 𝅘𝅥𝅭 𝅘𝅥𝅮 (1)

2 Pitch /15

2.1 (a) F♯   (b) A   (c) D   (7)

(d) C♯   (e) B♭   (f) G

(g) E

2.2 (4)

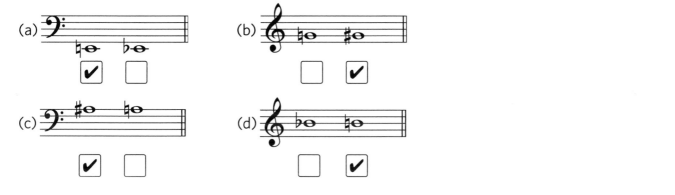

2.3 (a) 𝄢   (b) 𝄢   (c) 𝄞   (d) 𝄞 (4)

3 Keys and Scales /15

3.1 (1)

3.2 (1)

3.3 (3)

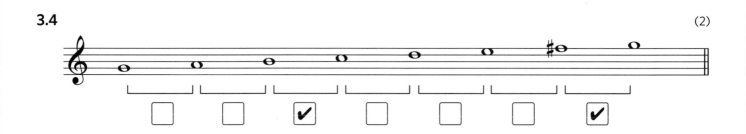

3.4 (2)

3.5 (a) **TRUE** (4)

(b) **TRUE**

(c) **FALSE**

(d) **TRUE**

3.6 (1)

3.7 FALSE (1)

3.8 (2)

4 Intervals

4.1   (5)

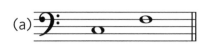   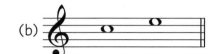   

   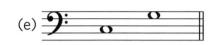

4.2 (a) 4th   (b) 6th   (c) 5th   (5)

(d) 7th   (e) 2nd

5 Tonic Triads

5.1 (a) **TRUE**   (3)

(b) **TRUE**

(c) **FALSE**

5.2   (3)

5.3 (a) G major   (4)

(b) F major

(c) C major

(d) D major

6 Terms and Signs   /5

♩ = 68 means: ⌢ means: ***pp*** means: (5)

68 crotchet beats in a minute   tie: hold for the value of   very quiet
                                 both notes

fine means: *cantabile* means:

the end   in a singing style

7 Music in Context   /5

7.1 **TRUE**   (1)

7.2 3   (1)

7.3 (a) dotted minim   (3)

   (b) bar 5

   (c) bar 6